Beginner's Guide to Pocket Watches

by

IAN BEILI

splat publishing ltd

Published by Splat Publishing Ltd
141b Lower Granton Road
Edinburgh
EH5 1EX

http://www.clocksmagazine.com

ISBN: 978 0 9562732 0 8

2 4 6 8 10 9 7 5 3

Printed by CBF Cheltenham Business Forms Ltd, 67 Hatherley Road, Cheltenham GL51 6EG

CONTENTS

Clocks Magazine Guides

No 1. Clock Repair, a Beginner's Guide
No 2. Beginner's Guide to Pocket Watches
No 3. American Clocks, An Introduction
No 4. What's it Worth? A Price Guide to Clocks 2014
No 5. Pocket Watches 1750-1920

INTRODUCTION

In this guide we will examine several of the different types of pocket watch likely to be encountered by the average collector at clock fairs, or offered for sale on Internet auction sites. For completeness we have included a watch from the 18th century, but have in the main concentrated on the more readily available watches from the 19th and 20th centuries.

Watchmakers regularly came up with improvements in design intended to enhance the reliability and accuracy of their watches. Unlike the cases and dials, which tended to be fairly standard over the years, watch mechanisms, known as 'movements', can vary considerably. Some mechanical features became synonymous with a particular period in the manufacturing process, and it is possible to tell a lot about a watch from the design and layout of the movement alone. Quite often a particular type of movement can add considerably to the value.

The development and historical context of the different types of watches will be discussed as we look at the watches individually. Many collectors of pocket watches are totally unconcerned with the mechanical aspect of their watches. However for the benefit of those who are, we will now give a brief description of the basic wheel train and the motionwork employed in a typical pocket watch movement.

(Note: Readers unfamiliar with some of the terminology, for example—'wheel train' or 'motionwork'—will find the Glossary at the end of this book helpful. Simplified line drawings of the wheel train and motionwork have been included here. In order to make the illustration easy to understand the wheel train is drawn showing the wheels and pinions arranged in a straight line, however in practice the wheels of a watch are configured differently in order to fit in the confines of the case. The relationship of the wheels is however exactly the same. The illustration of the motionwork is colour coded in order to help the beginner identify the components.)

In the diagram on the next page, you can see that a series of wheels (large gears) and pinions (small gears) known as the 'wheel train' drives another series of gears called the 'motionwork' which control the hands of the watch. The wheels of the wheel train are cut from brass and the pinions from steel. The gear wheels and pinions run on shafts known as 'arbors' contained between metal plates. On early movements the movement plates consist of a dial plate and a single top plate. Although referred to as the top plate, custom has it that the plate at the back of the watch (farthest from the dial) is called the top plate and the plate under the dial is called the dial plate. On later watches, a series of individually removable plates, referred to as 'bridges' and 'cocks', were used as opposed to a single top plate. A mainspring, which is a spiral spring contained in a 'barrel', is used to drive all pocket watches.

The mainspring powers the wheel train and ultimately the 'escape wheel' at the far end of the wheel train, which in turn gives power or 'impulse' to the 'pallets' of the escapement and thus to the 'balance wheel'. The pallets are a pair of specially shaped pawls that alternately intercept the teeth of the escape wheel. The balance wheel is not a gear wheel, but a spoked wheel which swings backwards and forwards at a rate controlled by

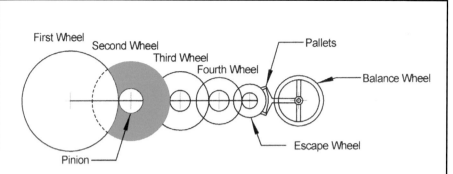

First Wheel
Second Wheel
Third Wheel
Fourth Wheel
Pallets
Balance Wheel
Escape Wheel
Pinion

The gearing of the wheel train and pinions, above, is designed so that the second wheel and pinion (green) rotates clockwise once every hour. The second wheel arbor is extended above the dial plate and the cannon pinion and pipe (red) is located on this arbor. The cannon pinion is made a tight positive fit on the second wheel arbor and forms part of the motionwork that drives the hour and minute hands of the watch. The motionwork, below, is therefore separate from the wheel train and situated between the dial plate and the dial. The minute hand is attached to the cannon pinion pipe that along with the second wheel rotates once every hour. The hour hand is attached to the hour wheel pipe (blue). The cannon pinion drives the hour wheel via the reverse minute wheel and pinion (yellow). The gearing between the cannon pinion, reverse wheel pinion and hour wheel provides for a 12:1 reduction and also ensures that the hour hand rotates concentrically with the minute hand once every 12 hours.

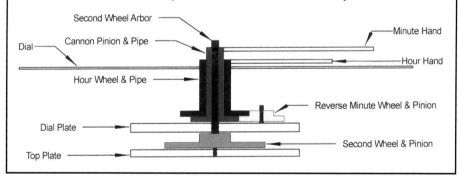

Second Wheel Arbor
Minute Hand
Dial
Cannon Pinion & Pipe
Hour Hand
Hour Wheel & Pipe
Reverse Minute Wheel & Pinion
Dial Plate
Second Wheel & Pinion
Top Plate

a fine spiral balance spring. The balance wheel therefore controls the rate at which the power of the mainspring is released through the escape wheel and hence the timekeeping of the watch. 'Escapement' is a term that refers to the combination of the escape wheel, pallets and balance wheel. Escapements changed over the years in the quest for better timekeeping and incorporated differently designed components in the process. The earliest watch escapements were 'verge' escapements followed by 'lever' and 'cylinder' escapements. These different escapements and components are discussed in the relevant chapters describing these particular types of watch. Irrespective of the type of escapement fitted to the watch the basic wheel train remained the same. There are of course many other important components incorporated in a watch movement, however these will all be discussed as and when they arise.

Many pocket watches are housed in silver or gold cases. If the cases are English in origin it is possible to tell from the hallmarks quite a bit about the watch. The hallmarks usually give us the date of manufacture, the initials of the silversmith who made the case and the city where the watch was assayed. Also, it is often found that the movements or dials of many 19th and early 20th century English pocket watches are inscribed with the name of the maker or retailer. Unfortunately however this is not always the case, especially with a lot of Swiss watches. This is a great pity, as the Swiss produced and exported thousands of pocket watches to England in the late 19th century and many of these watches are keenly collected today.

The Americans also exported vast quantities of pocket watches to England, principally at the end of the 19th century. With American watches we are much more fortunate. The majority of the leading American watch manufacturers developed an interesting habit of naming their watch movements as well as keeping records of the serial numbers of their watches. It is possible from these serial numbers to accurately date an American watch. The majority of American and Swiss pocket watches were imported and sold by High Street jewellers, whereas English watches were still being hand finished and assembled by the individual watchmaker who would sign the movement and retail the watch. The English watchmakers tended to be very conservative in both movement design and also in their methods of production.

As we look at the different types of watch, you will see how over the years the production methods and components employed by the Swiss, American and English watchmakers affected not only the movements and cases but also the marketing success of the different types of watch.

One of the principal differences in the late 19th century between the English and continental watch movements was in the use of the fusee and chain. In the 18th and 19th centuries mainsprings were made from steel which was not reliable in providing an even motive force. The spring would deliver a lot of power when first wound up, becoming less as the spring unwound, severely affecting the timekeeping qualities of the watch. The fusee is a component incorporated into many English clock and watch movements that equalises the power or torque of the mainspring to the movement train as it unwinds.

During the 19th century most British watchmakers were not watchmakers as such, but highly skilled watch finishers, who purchased semi-finished watch components from manufacturers primarily in London, Coventry and Prescot. The watchmaker would perhaps have one or two apprentices or would employ proficient out-workers to finish the majority of the components. Ultimately the 'maker' signed and retailed the finished watch but he did not actually *make* the watch in the true sense of the word.

Quite often young girls or children were employed by the watchmaker to assemble and finish the watches. Their delicate fingers and keen eyesight were considered a distinct advantage when working with small components. Records show that children as young as eight were employed in the making of components for watches.

American and Swiss watchmakers, on the other hand, quickly abandoned this approach to watchmaking, dispensing with the fusee and incorporating the much simpler 'going barrel' to power their movements. By the 1850s their entire production was geared to machine-made watches with interchangeable parts. This method of manufacture not only dramatically cut costs and speeded up production, but the movements could be made smaller and fitted into much less bulky cases. It was the reluctance of English watchmakers to change their methods of production and utilise the going barrel, which

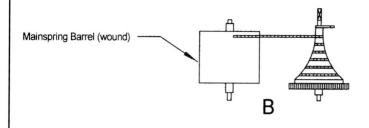

Mainspring Barrel (wound)

B

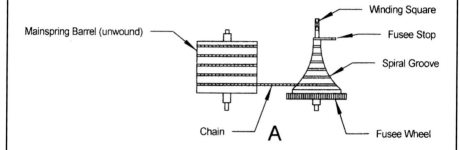

Mainspring Barrel (unwound)

Winding Square

Fusee Stop

Spiral Groove

Chain

A

Fusee Wheel

The fusee is conical in shape and incorporates a spiral groove to accommodate the fusee chain. The fusee wheel is attached to the fusee, which, in a fusee watch, is the first wheel in the watch train. The mainspring on a fusee watch is contained in a separate barrel. Inside the barrel, the outer end of the mainspring is attached to the inner wall of the barrel and the inner end of the spring hooks around the barrel arbor. The barrel arbor does not rotate and is held in place by a click and pawl. Whilst being wound the barrel rotates around the barrel arbor. Hooks at both ends of the fusee chain attach the chain to the barrel and fusee. With the mainspring inert in its unwound state the fusee chain is completely wound around the outer diameter of the barrel and the other end of the chain attached to the large diameter of the fusee *(A)*. In order to wind the mainspring a key is placed on the winding square of the fusee. As the fusee is wound the chain is transferred from the barrel to the fusee, running in the spiral groove of the fusee. A fusee stop is fitted to the fusee arbor, which in conjunction with a fusee stop lever prevents over winding.

When the mainspring is fully wound all the chain will have been transferred to the fusee.

In its wound-up state *(B)* the full force of the mainspring is applied via the chain to the smallest diameter of the fusee. As the watch runs, and the mainspring unwinds, the chain gradually transfers back to the unwinding barrel and the torque of the mainspring is transmitted to the progressively larger diameter of the fusee. The gradually changing diameter of the fusee compensates for the unequal force of the mainspring (torque x diameter) and provides for a constant and even transmission of power to the wheel train in the process.

Figure 1.

led to the decline and eventual collapse of the English watchmaking industry.

Irrespective of the type of movement or where the watch was manufactured, visually most mid 19th and early 20th century pocket watch cases fall into three distinct styles or patterns, unlike the 18th and early 19th century verge watches that were usually housed in 'pair' cases, literally two separate cases. This type of case is seldom seen much after the 1840s.

We will look at an interesting pair-cased verge watch in the first chapter, but first we will take a look at some of the more common 19th and 20th century cases encountered by the average collector. It should be remembered that watch case making was an art in itself. The watchmaker would buy cases from the case maker who would provide a range of suitable sizes and designs popular at the time.

Figures 1 and **2** show a 'hunter' and 'half-hunter' case. With the hunter case (on the right in the illustration) the entire dial and movement is encased. In order to tell the time the hinged front of the case has to be opened. This type of case was designed to protect both the dial and movement from damage, as might happen, for example, when the

Figure 2.

Figure 3.

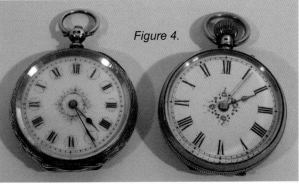

Figure 4.

wearer was out hunting, hence the name.

The half-hunter (on the left) is a compromise between the hunter and open dial watch shown in **figure 3.** With the half-hunter a small crystal or lunette is placed in the centre of the case making it possible to tell the time at a glance without opening the front. This opens in the same way as the hunter revealing the whole dial. These are both 'stem-wind' watches. The movement is wound up and the hands adjusted by a grooved 'crown' attached to a 'stem' at the top of the case. All pocket watches have a circular bow and pendant at the top of the case on to which a watch chain could be attached.

Many 19th century Swiss and English watches, such as that shown in **figure 3,** were wound using a separate small watch key. You will notice the absence of the knurled winding crown at the top. On most key-wind watches the movement is wound from the back, the back cover being hinged to reveal the winding square, and the hands adjusted by opening the front of the watch and placing the key on a small square formed on the fulcrum of the minute hand.

The three watches shown in **figures 1** to **3** were made and worn by men, however by the 1880s smaller pocket or fob watches started to be made especially for women. **Figure 4** shows two typical Swiss ladies' fob watches. These watches are generally housed in open dial cases but it is possible to come across hunter and half-hunter examples. Both the dials and cases are, as you would expect, more decorative. The cases were heavily engraved, often with floral motifs. These watches were designed to be visu-ally admired and to be attached to blouses and dresses. They were worn in the manner of jewellery rather than being obscured in a gentleman's waistcoat pocket.

The decorative dials on these small Swiss fob watches can become the subject of a col-lection in themselves and **figure 5** shows a range of mass-produced Swiss watch dials, all of them slightly different.

Figure

CHAPTER 1
An 18ᵗʰ century pair-cased verge watch

Henry Hindley is a well-known 18ᵗʰ century maker of quality clocks and watches. Born in 1701 and working in Wigan and then York from 1731 until his death in 1771, Hindley was a prolific and inventive maker, greatly respected and admired both as a clockmaker and instrument maker. The pair-cased verge watch shown here is by Henry Hindley.

The verge movement was one of the earliest types of movement fitted to pocket watches and this watch is a very good example of this particular type of mid-18ᵗʰ century movement. The watch is shown in **figures 6** and **7** and as you can see the outer case is made from tortoiseshell. **Figure 8** shows the watch removed from its outer case and you can see the movement is housed in a gilt case. Although the dial has unfortunately been slightly damaged at some time you can see it is written with Roman numerals for the hours and smaller Arabic numerals for the minutes, very typical of the period.

By the 1750s, with the adoption of the balance spring, watches were becoming much more accurate; and it was felt the timekeeping had improved sufficiently to record the minutes on the dial. The original beetle-and-poker style hands are very well executed and finished.

Early verge pair-cased watches were housed in cases covered in many different materials: shagreen, horn, tortoiseshell and leather to name but a few, as well as the more traditional silver, gilt or gold. Later 19th century pair-cased watches were predominantly

Figure 6.

Figure 7.

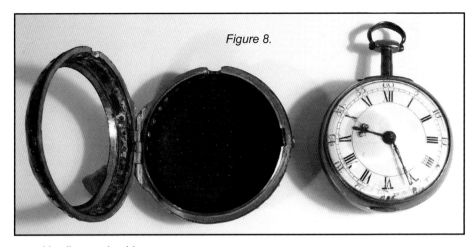

Figure 8.

cased in silver and gold cases.

The verge watch takes its name from one of the main components employed in the escapement of the movement.

The actual verge is an arbor with a pair of pallets or flags. This arbor is attached to the balance wheel; on most watches it is generally termed the 'balance staff'. The pallets on the verge arbor alternately intercept the teeth of the escape wheel which, on a verge watch is referred to as the 'crown' wheel because the shape of the teeth. They are upright rather than radial and are cut in the rim of the wheel. The small crown wheel is set at right angles to the rest of the wheel train. A small toothed cog or 'pinion' on the crown wheel axle or 'arbor' meshes with a contrate wheel. The contrate wheel, like the crown wheel, has upright teeth cut in the rim of the wheel.

An English verge watch always employs a fusee and chain. Early verge movements always had all the wheelwork between a plate at the front and another at the back of the watch. Later verge watches sometimes had a separate 'bridge', a separate plate which allowed for easy removal of the mainspring barrel.

Figure 9.

Figure 10.

Figure 11.

Figure 12.

On early verge movements the 'balance cock' which supports the top pivot of the balance wheel was exceptionally large and highly engraved and pierced, partly for decoration and partly to protect the large steel balance wheel. With later movements the balance cock is solid, smaller and less elaborately decorated and as a result the balance wheel is more exposed. When viewed from the side of the movement the contrate wheel with its upright teeth is the most recognisable feature of a verge movement.

A verge escapement is known as a frictional rest recoil escapement. Although a robust and reliable escapement, the constant contact and friction between the pallets and the teeth of the crown wheel affects the operation of the balance and hence the timekeeping of the watch.

The movement is removed through the front of the case by opening the dial bezel and releasing the sprung catch at the bottom of the dial. **Figure 9** shows the movement swung out of its case. The large pierced balance cock and elaborately engraved movement plate on this watch is shown in **figure 10**. This watch has a full-plate movement with a silver regulator to adjust the balance spring and the timekeeping of the watch. The engraving on both the balance cock and the movement plate is very fine and a small hand with a pointing finger has been engraved next to the regulator disc in order to indicate the amount of regulation. The large fan-shaped foot of the balance cock is typical of the period as well as the engraving of a grotesque mask, a very popular decorative motif in the 18th century. The engraving of the plate is purely decorative and can take many forms.

Figure 11 shows the fusee and just to the side of the fusee the very ornate fusee stop pivot. In **figure 12** the contrate wheel is shown. **Figures 11** and **12** also show the square baluster movement pillars which separate the plates.

These square decorative pillars are again a typical feature of a mid-18th century verge watch. The contrate wheel is however still the most easily identifiable component of a verge movement.

Even though this watch is signed by a highly respected maker, it is however still very similar to many other 18th century pocket watch movements of the period.

The movement from a slightly later silver pair-cased verge watch is shown in **figures 13** and **14**. The silver case from this watch is hallmarked 1806 and a comparison with the Hindley movement reveals one or two differences. The movement is still regulated

Figure 13.

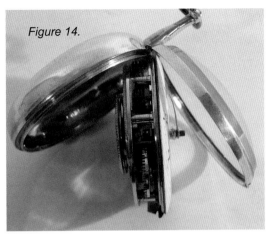

Figure 14.

by a Tompion regulator, but the foot of the balance cock is now much smaller and the movement top plate less ornate. Only the retailer's name is engraved on the movement plate. The movement pillars shown in **figure 14** are now cylindrical and the movement much slimmer and less bulky.

Unlike the 19th century there is very little information on the watchmaking practices of the 17th and early 18th century and it is difficult to know how much of the finished watch was the actual work of the watchmaker who signed and retailed the watch.

It is thought that most watchmakers especially in provincial cities and towns would buy in the movements or components. With the aid of apprentices the watchmaker would then possibly finish and adjust the movements before finally assembling, casing and retailing the watch.

By the middle of the 18th century and onwards many complete watches were being bought from the main clockmaking centres in London, Coventry, Birmingham and Prescot.

The watchmaker's name would appear on the movement; he would sell the watch but not necessarily have made the watch or had anything to do with the manufacture of the watch.

CHAPTER 2
An English open-dial silver pocket watch

The second watch I would like to describe is a little unusual and is perhaps a good example to illustrate what we can deduce from both a watch movement and its case. The English open dial silver pocket watch shown in **figure 15** is fitted with a small verge movement. This movement is a very late example with no decorative engraving to the movement plate and a very plain un-pierced balance cock.

The movement is numbered 2630 and is housed in a single or consular case, which bears the Birmingham hallmark for 1896. The maker is also a little unusual in that the watch is signed by Sarah Woodgates, a lady watchmaker.

With later verge movements such as this, the balance cock is un-pierced, smaller and undecorated. The balance cock no longer fully protects the balance wheel which is much more exposed.

When viewed from the side of the movement the contrate wheel with its upright teeth can be seen and this is still the most recognisable feature of a verge movement.

Verge movements are always key-wound. The hands are adjusted by opening the dial bezel and placing the key on a square provided to adjust the minute hand.

The movement is removed through the front of the case by opening the dial bezel and releasing the sprung catch at the bottom of the dial. **Figure 16** shows the movement swung out of its case. The small jewelled balance cock and broad steel balance wheel on this watch is shown in **figure 17**; you can clearly see the movement top plate with the

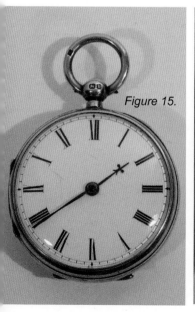

Figure 15.

Figure 16.

Figure 17.

maker's signature engraved on it. This watch is a full plate movement with a separate bridge for the mainspring barrel. With this watch, unlike the earlier verge watch, a Bosley regulation lever adjusts the balance spring and the timekeeping of the watch. The top plate is engraved with a fast-and-slow scale in order to help regulate the watch. As a comparison, **figure 18** shows two balance cocks from earlier verge watches.

Here the balance cocks are not only larger but also highly decorative and pierced. The decoration is such that balance cocks from discarded movements are now highly sought after and collected in their own right!

Our verge watch, viewed from the side of the movement, **figure 19**, shows the contrate wheel and fusee. It is also possible to see one of the round movement pillars separating the plates. Early 18th century verge watches tended to have bulky square pillars and the movement components tended to be quite a bit larger.

To find a verge movement in a single case dated 1896 is certainly uncommon and you would be right in initially wondering if the movement had been re-cased at some time.

Given the small size of the movement, its features and condition I do not personally think this is the case. However unfortunately I have been unable to find any trace of Sarah Woodgates in any of the standard reference books on watchmakers which would help in confirming a date for the movement.

Quite often female watchmakers were not practising watchmakers in the accepted sense. Many were watchmakers' widows, who kept the family business running after the demise of their late husband.

Although by the last quarter of the 19th century the English lever watch was being produced by most watch manufacturers and considered far superior in timekeeping to

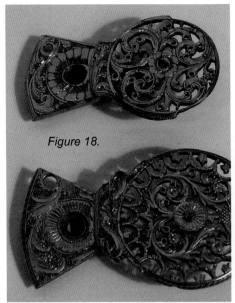

Figure 18.

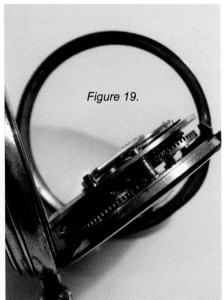

Figure 19.

the to the verge watch, it does not necessarily follow that all watchmakers/manufacturers considered the verge movement as outdated and abandon production completely. The verge movement was still in common use during the 19th century; it was robust, reliable and easy to make and repair.

Several collectors and dealers with many years experience of pocket watches have examined the watch and case and they are all of the opinion that both case and movement could possibly have started life together. The movement and dial fit and line up exactly and no part of the case shows any signs of having being altered. The movement also shows only very slight signs of wear and has not been repaired at all.

The majority of 18th and 19th century verge watches exhibit quite lot of wear and have been repaired several times over the years.

A number of late verge watches such as this one have come to light and many authorities now consider that the production of verge watches may have continued for a far longer period than was previously considered to be the case.

This watch runs very well and keeps good time … for a verge!

CHAPTER 3
An English lever pocket watch

The English lever pocket watch became the standard watch produced by the majority of English watchmakers during the mid-nineteenth and early twentieth century. The accuracy of the lever movement far superseded that of the verge watch which started to go out of production during the second half of the nineteenth century. **Figure 20** shows a typical open-dial English lever watch. The single case is hallmarked Birmingham 1907 and the watch movement is inscribed 'Wm. Kirby, Malton'. Lever watches are normally found housed in single cases.

The movement and dial both carry the serial number 20824 and the large Roman numerals and small recessed seconds dial are all typical features of a watch of this period. Although William Kirby is not listed in Brian Loomes' WATCHMAKERS AND CLOCKMAKERS OF THE WORLD (21st Century Edition), the Kirby family of watchmakers, a prolific family of watchmakers in the East Riding of Yorkshire especially in the Malton and Driffield areas, is listed. It is a strong probability that William was a member of this family, possibly one of the last to sell and make watches in Malton.

As with the verge watch, the English lever takes its name from the escapement fitted to the watch, this time from the lever on to which the pallets are attached.

The English clockmaker and watchmaker Thomas Mudge is credited with the invention of the detached lever escapement somewhere around the 1770s. However it was not perfected until around 1830.

The lever is situated between the escape wheel and the balance wheel and as the teeth of the escape wheel impulse the pallets, the lever impulses the balance wheel

Figure 20.

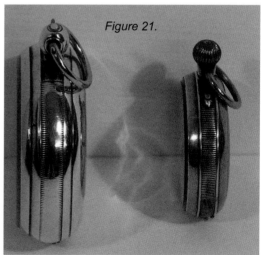

Figure 21.

Figure 22.

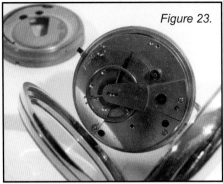

Figure 23.

which in turn determines the rate of the watch. As the lever and pallets are detached from the balance wheel, the lever does not impede or affect the efficiency of the balance or its timekeeping qualities.

With the English lever, as opposed to the Swiss lever, the layout of the escapement is such that the balance wheel, lever and pallets are situated at right angles to the escape wheel: the three components are laid out in a triangular formation. This layout was greatly favoured by English watchmakers of the period. English lever watches always incorporate the fusee, requiring bulky heavier cases to house the movements.

Figure 21 shows two 19th century pocket watches: that on the left is an English watch with a fusee movement and that on the right a Swiss watch which dispensed with the fusee and incorporated a going barrel. Utilising the going barrel not only reduced the cost of the watch but also made it possible to manufacture much smaller and lighter watches. There can be little doubt that these were primary reasons why Swiss watches became increasingly popular with the watch-buying public. The English lever watch shown in **figure 20** is key-wound and the back of the case is opened in order to access winding arbor. The hands are adjusted with the key by opening the dial bezel and adjusting the square on the minute hand with the key.

Figure 24.

Figure 25.

The movement is removed from the case in the same way as the verge watch. The dial bezel is opened and the sprung catch at the bottom of the dial is released. The movement can then be swung out from the case.

Figure 22 shows the movement free of the case. As this watch is key-wound and the back of the case would be opened fairly frequently in order to wind the watch, a dust cap was fitted to try and prevent dirt and dust from entering the movement. The movement with the dust cap removed can be seen in **figure 23** and you can see that the rear of the movement appears very similar to the late verge watch that we looked at in Chapter 2.

The movement is fitted with a bridge for the mainspring barrel and the balance cock is solid and undecorated. A much lighter gold balance wheel is fitted as opposed to the heavier steel balance wheel fitted to verge watches. A regulation lever adjusts the timekeeping of the watch.

A side view of the movement in **figure 24** shows the fusee and you can just see the small ratchet for the maintaining power. Maintaining power was a refinement fitted to quality fusee watches. The maintaining power was in effect a temporary motive power which kept the movement running whilst the watch was being wound, maintaining its accuracy.

The watch shown in **figures 25** and **26** is also an English fusee lever watch, only here both the case and dial are made from silver. The dial in particular has been very well decorated. It has raised numerals in gold in order to make them stand out from the rest of the dial.

Although a refined watch and slightly less bulky than the watch shown in **figure 20** it is still quite large due to the fusee movement. Despite their size and price these were quality watches and excellent timekeepers. It was for this reason that the English watchmakers were very reluctant to change the design.

With English watches the components were predominantly hand finished and the parts were not therefore interchangeable. Swiss and American manufacturers, on the other hand, pioneered mass production and the use of interchangeable parts. This greatly reduced the manufacturing costs of their watches. Unfortunately the public did not always appreciate the virtues of the English watch and were only too ready to purchase the cheaper Swiss and American models which were being imported at the time. Ultimately this led to the demise of watchmaking in England.

Figure 26.

CHAPTER 4
An Swiss open-dial pocket watch

The dial of the late 19th century Swiss open dial silver pocket watch shown in **figures 27** and **28** boasts not only the name of the retailer but also the fact that the movement possesses a 'non-magnetic lever'. The watch is branded as 'The Trusty' and was retailed by T Fattorini, a very large consortium of watch and jewellery retailers in the North of England.

This type of watch, a type British watchmakers were unwilling to make, was the beginning of the end for watchmaking in the Britain. Prior to its introduction, pocket watches had been a luxury item affordable only to the middle-classes and the affluent. But between 1880 and 1890 the market had tripled and by the end of this period the wealth of the nation had created a new class of customer, a customer who could not only afford a watch like this but also needed a reliable portable timepiece.

By the 1890s, Swiss and American watch manufacturers were producing thousands of these mass-produced watches and exporting them to Britain and the rest of Europe. Retailing at around half the price of the British watches of the period, the British watchmakers were left with little option but to pack up and go out of business. The new watch-buying public were keen to obtain the latest up-to-date watches and the retailers and manufacturers were not slow in advertising the latest improvements on the dials of their watches.

Watches became a status symbol very much like mobile phones today; you had to have the latest most advanced model available. Very few members of the public would be aware of the true advantage of a 'non-magnetic lever', a 'safety pinion' or a 'detached lever'—or any of the other features advertised on the dials of these watches—but as a marketing ploy it worked very well.

Figure 27.

Figure 28.

Figure 29.

Figure 30.

Figure 31.

Although visually the watch shown in **figure 27** is very similar to the English lever watch we saw in Chapter 3, mechanically, it is different in a number of ways. In **figure 29** you can see the case with one of the double doors open, and although the watch is still key-wound, the layout and design of the movement is radically different. You can see the two keyholes in the back of the double hinged case. With this watch not only is the movement wound up but the hands are also set from the back of the case. This new method of hand-adjustment meant that in was no longer necessary to provide a hinged dial bezel. On this watch the dial bezel is a positive snap fit, and the movement is removed through the rear of the case, as opposed to being swung out through the front. This watch still retains a dust cap to prevent dirt entering the movement as can be seen in **figure 30.**

More radical changes from the previous watches we have looked at can be seen in **figure 31**. With the dust cap removed you can see the balance wheel and balance cock is placed between the movement plates. This type of movement is known as a three-quarter-plate movement. In both the English verge and lever full-plate movements the balance wheel was placed above the movement plate, necessitating a much thicker case. By re-designing the layout and relationship of the wheels and escapement and by placing the balance wheel between the movement plates it was possible to produce a slimmer more practical watch.

Another equally important factor was the adoption of the going barrel as opposed to the fusee. As the reliability and quality of mainsprings had improved, American and Swiss watch manufacturers had realised a fusee was no longer necessary for an accurate watch. This made these new watches much cheaper to produce and far easier to assemble.

This watch is fitted with a lever escapement, however both the Americans and Swiss adopted a different layout to the English lever, placing the balance wheel, lever and escape wheel in a straight line.

The design of the escape wheel also changed. The English lever escapement used an escape wheel with thin acutely angled and pointed teeth. The design of the teeth and the angle of the pallets were such that only the lever provided the impulse to the balance wheel. With the Swiss straight-line lever escapement, the escape wheel teeth were much broader and club shaped. Here, the design of the escape wheel teeth and the pallets combined with the lever to impulse the balance. This design reduced wear to the escape wheel and improved accuracy.

Improvements in metallurgy and a better understanding of the properties of metals resulted in more suitable materials being used and incorporated into the movement and components. Better quality Swiss watches incorporated the bimetallic balance wheel fitted with compensation and timing screws in order to counteract the effects of temperature change on the rate of the balance.

The combination of improved materials, design and marketing created a whole new concept in both the retailing and purchasing of pocket watches. This type of watch was the first truly affordable and accurate watch available to the general public. Although many of these watches are now over 100 years old, they are still capable of accurate and reliable timekeeping.

The role of the traditional watchmaker also changed. No longer would the watchmaker assemble or finish the watches. Complete watches would be bought in and retailed by the 'watchmaker', with his name on the dial. This in turn led to a much wider range of watches being offered for sale, and the beginning of the commercial high street jeweller.

CHAPTER 5
An American pocket watch

For a long period the market for pocket watches was dominated by English and Swiss manufacturers, but in the late 19th century—when American watchmakers started exporting well-made and affordable watches to England and Europe—this was to change.

The Americans were relative newcomers to watchmaking, and over the years had noted the advances made by the Swiss and European watchmakers of the period. They could see that the future of the watchmaking industry would be reliant upon the mass-production of watches with interchangeable parts. American watchmaking really got going in 1850 with the partnership of Aaron Dennison, Edward Howard and Samuel

Figure 32.

Curtis who together formed what was to become the Waltham Watch Company. Several other American firms subsequently sprang into existence, the most notable and successful being Elgin and Waterbury. The American watches were sold in a variety of case styles, made from gold and silver. Cheaper cases were gold-filled. Not only were the movement components interchangeable but standardisation of movement sizes meant that the cases and movements could be interchanged as well. It was therefore possible for the retailer to choose movements and cases to suit a given budget, a novel idea at the time, and extremely popular with public and retailer alike.

Another original idea adopted by many American firms was that of naming the different types of movement they manufactured: the Giant, the Warren, the Ellery, the Yankee, the Columbus, to name but a few. Sometimes the name referred to an owner or partner of the company or sometimes to a specific attribute of the movement of the watch.

Waltham and Elgin were good quality American watches which nearly always employed the Swiss in-line lever escapement as well as a going barrel; a lot of the movements were substantially jewelled. All the Waltham watch movements carry serial numbers which were recorded by the manufacturers. From these serial numbers it is possible to date the approximate year of manufacture.

The vast majority of American pocket watches encountered by the collector are stem-wound, as opposed to being wound with a key. The Swiss watchmaker Louis Audemars introduced stem winding for both winding the watch and setting the hands in 1838. By the end of the 19th century most continental and American watches employed this method of winding which was not compatible with a fusee movement. Only the English watchmakers who still insisted on making fusee movements employed key winding right up to the 20th century. Stem winding was a far more convenient means of winding and setting the hands of a pocket watch, yet another reason for the decline in popularity and sales of the English pocket watches of the period.

Waltham & Co manufactured all of the three pocket watches shown in **figures 32** and **33**. These watches are all of the same size but fitted into different cases, all unadorned. These became the standard practical men's timepieces of the day.

The hunter watch (Serial No: 19400047, dated 1913/14) is housed in a gold-filled case, as is one of the open-dial watches (Serial No: 24083144, dated 1921/22). The other open-dial watch is fitted into a silver case hallmarked in Birmingham in 1898 (Serial No: 8142490, dated 1897/8).

Clearly the movement in the silver case had been imported and cased in England, however it would be just as easy to transfer the movement from the other open-dial

Figure 33.

watch into this silver case if so wished.

Because the watches are stem-wound, the dial bezels are all a snap fit on the case. None of the movements was fitted with a dust cap, but all the cases were provided with a second tightly fitting case door to keep dust out.

Figure 34 shows the movements of the three watches: you can see there is very little difference between them. A close-up of one is shown in **figure 35.** All have Swiss in-line lever escapements and balance wheels fitted with compensation and timing screws. These movements are generally referred to as 'half-plate': separate plates or bridges are used to locate the train wheels and going barrels. As usual, the balance wheel is located by its own cock.

By further breaking down the plates of the movement the designers made it much easier to assemble the watches. Not only did this speed up production but also aided the routine servicing of the watches.

Although a far cry from the days of the expensive highly decorated verge watches of the 18th century, the movement plates do carry a certain amount of engine turned decoration which conveys the impression of quality.

These well-made reliable watches were being produced at a time when the

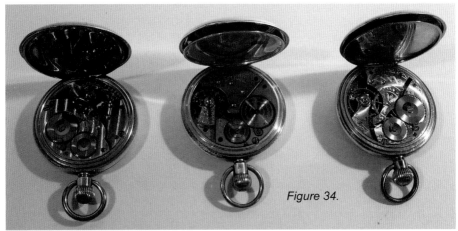

Figure 34.

Figure 35.

economy of most large industrial countries was changing from being agriculturally based to industrial. Thousands of people were migrating from the country to the towns in search of work and prosperity; their new working lifestyles with regulated working hours and shift patterns required accurate watches in order for them to earn their living. Like the people who owned watches, the watch had moved on, and was no longer just a curiosity or a luxury toy for the wealthy.

CHAPTER 6
A ladies' fob watch

The watches we have looked at in previous chapters were designed for men. In this chapter we will look at three ladies' watches, made not just as timepieces but as items of decorative jewellery.

By the late 19th and early 20th centuries the general prosperity of the leading manufacturing countries had increased substantially. The increased prosperity was also starting to percolate down to the lower levels of society. People were on the whole better educated and becoming more conscious of their social responsibilities. Also, women of all classes were beginning to play a much more important role in both the community and the working life of the nation. Women were no longer considered subservient to men and were being admitted to the world of medicine, education and social reform.

As the status of women generally rose in society, so too did their individual wealth. Many women were no longer reliant on generous husbands purchasing items for personal use. Although watches were still quite expensive, they were not beyond the means of the average middle-class lady of the day. Watchmakers realised that a whole new market was opening up to them, requiring new watches. These would have to be designed with feminine taste in mind, and for practical reasons made much smaller than the conventional pocket watch of the day.

As was customary, most men in the 18th and 19th centuries—as well as the opening decades of the 20th—would wear a waistcoat or vest. The pocket watch was carried in a small pocket specifically provided in the garment for that purpose. The watch was not on view until the owner wished to tell the time and removed the watch from his pocket.

Women, on the other hand, did not wear waistcoats: the small ladies fob watches were usually pinned to their blouses or dresses, and remained permanently on view. The fob is the small chain or ribbon used to attach the watch to the clothing.

Figure 36.

Fob watches quickly became a fashion accessory as much as anything else, and these ladies watches were usually delicately engraved, especially around the side and rear door of the case. The movements were usually housed in open-dial cases, but it is possible to find hunter and half-hunter cases in gold, silver and enamel. The dials were much more colourful and sometimes semi-precious stones were set in the dial to highlight both the chapter ring and the numerals.

The Swiss watchmakers in particular

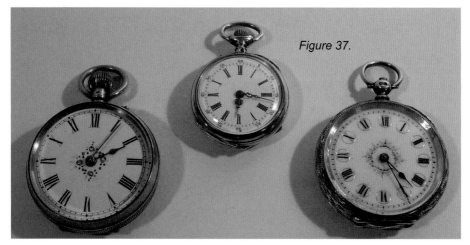

Figure 37.

were very quick to exploit the new market unfolding before them and the three small silver watches shown in **figures 36**, **37** and **38** are typical Swiss ladies fob watches of the period.

The dial shown in **figure 36** is very pretty (as most of these dials were). At its centre are delicate small flowers and the numerals have been circled in gold. These watches were exported to England by the thousand and are now keenly collected. The earlier fob watches tended to be key wound, but the vast majority of later fob watches tend to be stem wound. **Figures 39** and **40** show the movements of the watches, and although you do find three-quarter plate movements as shown in **figure 39**, most movements have separate bridges and cocks to retain all the wheelwork. The movement shown in **figure 40** would be regarded as a typical key-wound 'Geneva bar' movement, the 'bars' being the small plates used to hold the individual wheels.

The better quality watches were jewelled, and nearly all employ a cylinder escapement. George Graham who worked with perhaps the greatest English clockmaker Thomas Tompion (and was married to his niece) first introduced the

Figure 38.

cylinder escapement in 1726, and although cylinder escapements are found in English watches it was the Swiss watchmakers who used the escapement most extensively in these small fob watches. The cylinder escapement is named after the hollow cylinder fitted into the balance wheel staff.

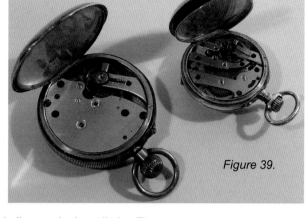

Figure 39.

The escape wheel teeth are cut with a sloping impulse face, which engages with both the outside and inside lips of the hollow cut in the cylinder. The escape wheel teeth impulse the cylinder/balance wheel twice per vibration. Although very efficient when new, the escapement is prone to wear owing to the amount of friction between the lips of the cylinder and the teeth of the escape wheel.

Figure 40.

Most of these watches are now well over 100 years old and even though they may not have been in continuous use, the escapements are now very badly worn and they tend to keep rather poor time.

For this reason most of these watches are now collected for their visual appeal and intrinsic value rather than the interest of the movements.

Over the years the fob watches became progressively more delicate and smaller in size. **Figure 41** shows a late silver fob watch and you can see it is not much larger than a one-penny piece! Once movements could be made a small as this it was only a matter of time before the cases were adapted and the wristwatch was born.

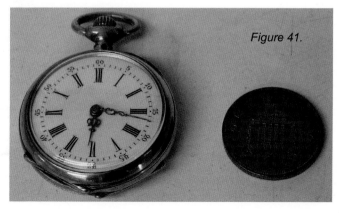

Figure 41.

CHAPTER 7
A quarter-repeating watch

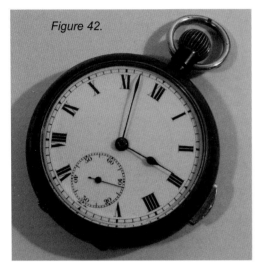

Figure 42.

The watch we are going to look at in this chapter is distinctively different from all the other watches that we have looked at so far. In fact this watch movement has more in common with a clock than a traditional watch, so much so that these watches were originally called 'clock-watches' when first made.

Initially, looking at the watch shown in **figure 42,** there seems to be very little difference between this and a standard stem-wound pocket watch from the early 20th century. However closer examination reveals a brass button or push-piece protruding from the side of the case at the three o'clock position. If the push-piece is pressed the difference in the watches is immediately apparent as the watch proceeds to strike the last hour and quarters.

These watches are now known as quarter repeaters, and the Swiss quarter repeater shown in **figure 42** is housed in a gunmetal case and was made around 1915. Today the majority of striking watches or watches that audibly tell the time are usually made for people who are visually impaired, but in reality striking watches date back as far as the 16th century.

This may be because the very early clocks in abbeys and churches were audible rather than visual … remember the word 'clock' is derived from 'cloche', the French word for 'bell'.

The English clockmaker Edward Barlow (1636-1716) invented the rack striking system employed in striking watches right up to the present day, however another English clockmaker, Daniel Quare (1649-1724), is credited with developing the repeater mechanism and took out several patents.

The early repeating watches struck the hours and quarters on small bells, but in 1783 French horologist Abraham-Louis Breguet invented the 'gong-spring' which replaced the bells in watches. The gongs were struck with small independent hammers, the gongs being carefully coiled around the inside of the case, tuned and adjusted for both pitch and volume.

Pressing the push-piece in effect winds the spring of the striking train and provides the energy for the operation of the strike. The power is released by a centrifugal governor that controls the speed of the striking. The striking of the hours and quarters is controlled by a number of complex detents or levers, which act on the hour and quarter snails that in turn are driven by the watch movement.

With a quarter repeater there are usually two gongs struck by separate hammers. The tuning of the two gong springs produces a 'ting-tang' sound. When depressing the push-piece the last hours are first struck on one gong, followed by one ting-tang for each quarter-hour past the hour. As an example, at ten to ten the hour gong would sound nine times, indicating that it was past nine o'clock, the two gongs (ting-tang) would then be struck three times indicating it was past 9.45. You could then deduce the time was somewhere between quarter to ten and ten o'clock.

Figure 43 shows the movement and you can see the centrifugal governor, which controls the speed of the strike. You can also see the hammers and steel gongs coiled around the inside edge of the case.

The gilded movement is similar to a Geneva bar, with separate cocks for the escape and fourth wheels. The centre and third wheels are fitted to the barrel bridge. The movement is fully jewelled and the escapement is a Swiss lever.

Figure 43.

As watchmaking developed much more sophisticated movements were made and five-minute and minute repeaters became prevalent. English maker Thomas Mudge (1715-1794) is credited with making the first minute repeater as early as 1750. This is the most advanced of repeating watches, striking the hours, quarters and minutes.

Today there is very little practical use for watches that strike the hours, but in 1915, and for many years before that these watches would have been of great value in determining the time after dark. Most domestic houses were not lit with electricity until the 1920s and if you needed to see the time after 'lights out' it would have been necessary to strike a match or light a candle in order to do so. Quite an involved and even dangerous thing to do, especially if you were half-asleep!

A watch that struck and repeated the hours would have been considered a valuable and useful asset rather than a novelty or whim. These were never cheap, and are more frequently found in silver and gold cases. Gunmetal would be the cheapest case available and with this watch the practical use of the watch would have taken precedence over cosmetic pride. The mechanical attributes of the watch far outweigh the worth of the case, which must have been of prime consideration to the original owner.

CHAPTER 8
A collector's guide

Figure 44.

There is a vast range of watches to collect, and one of the problems in writing this book has been deciding what to include and what to leave out. We hope that the descriptions did not dwell on the technical attributes of the watches too much, but were sufficiently detailed and informed to enable the collector to spot and understand the essential mechanical differences between the watches.

If nothing else this book may have stimulated an interest in pocket watches and some readers may now consider collecting pocket watches as a hobby. We have shown typical examples from each of the main types of watch encountered by the average collector, watches easily obtained and still in plentiful supply. Most of these watches are still affordable in comparison with other collectable antiques and clocks. The only watches that are perhaps beyond the collector of modest means would be watches from the early to mid 18th century, but there are plenty of collectable 19th century watches that are still quite reasonably priced.

Of course, the diversity of watches on offer to the collector goes far beyond the range of watches shown in this book and readers should be aware that there are many variations in movements, escapements, dials and cases.

It is very important to recognise any differences in the movements, as any variation from the norm can effect the value of the watch. To many people all pocket watches look the same, the only exception being pair-cased watches, which clearly are a bit different. It is therefore possible for the knowledgeable collector to spot something the seller has missed, and get a bargain in the process.

Condition is all-important. If the movement is not working it can be very expensive—

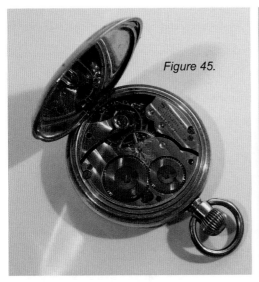

Figure 45.

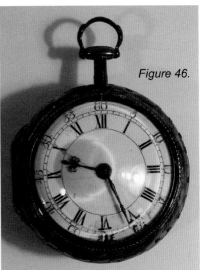

Figure 46.

even prohibitive—to have it repaired. Damaged dials are perhaps one of the most detrimental and expensive of faults. As a watch is quite small the eye focuses on the dial and a disfigured or badly cracked dial detracts from the overall appearance and value of a watch. On the whole case repairs are not as expensive or difficult to arrange. Always ensure that the movement is original to the case, especially with early movements that may have been re-cased at some time.

As with all collectable items, you must be prepared to pay more for rarer watches or watches with unusual one-off features. This can be money well spent in the long run,

Figure 47.

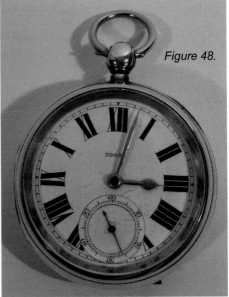

Figure 48.

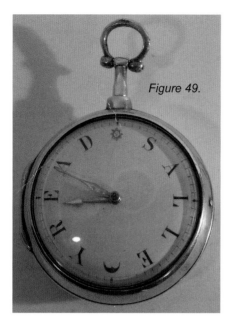

Figure 49.

as generally speaking these watches are always of interest to the serious collector wishing to make his or her collection a little more unique.

For the beginner it is always difficult to know what to collect, especially at first. Watches are personal items which reflect your personal preferences and taste. A good introduction to pocket watch collecting could be the Swiss ladies fob watches shown in **figure 44** and discussed in Chapter 6. I know many collectors who started collecting pocket watches by simply being attracted to the colourful dials and decorative cases of these small watches.

With their cylinder movements and thin silver cases these watches are still not expensive and can represent very good value for money. Here the diversification and interest is in the cases and dials rather than the movements. These watches are frequently seen in second-hand jewellery shops. If the retailer does not specialise in watches and the watch has an unusual movement the seller may not fully appreciate the value of what he or she is selling. Generally at the time of writing these watches in good condition can be bought for around £80-£90. Expect to pay more if the case is fully engraved or the dial is multicoloured and inset with decorative stones.

American watches discussed in Chapter 5 are another field of specialisation. Here the challenge is to collect not only the different types of movement available but also watches from the many different manufacturers.

Figure 50.

Watchmaking in the USA was a precarious business in the 19th century and many firms failed or were taken over in what was a highly competitive market.

Some manufacturers were only in business for a few years before going into liquidation or being bought out and collectors keenly seek their watches if they come on the market. On the other hand large firms such as Waltham and Elgin produced thousands of watches over a long period and the many different models can be interesting to collect. There is a lot of information available on American watches and this in itself can make collecting these watches very interesting and rewarding.

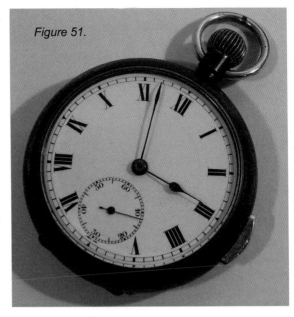

Figure 51.

American watches were produced in gold, silver and alloy cases and the price of the watches nowadays will reflect this. The watch in **figure 45** is housed in a gold-filled case and you would not expect to have to pay more than £100 for such a watch in good condition. If the case were solid gold or silver you would expect to pay proportionately more.

Another possibility is to collect watches from the different periods of watchmaking, encompassing as many of the different types of movement that have been used as you can afford. This would be a much harder and more expensive task if you were to include all the possible variations on offer. It would however be possible to collect one of each of the more common variants without breaking the bank—a verge, an English lever, a Swiss lever, an English cylinder and Swiss cylinder. Rarer escapements are available, but at a price!

Pair-cased verge watches from the 18th century such as that discussed in Chapter 1 and shown in **figure 46** tend to be rather expensive, even in poor condition, however early 18th century examples are still in reasonable supply and standard examples are not prohibitively priced. Expect to pay around £360-£380 for a William IV silver pair-cased verge in good condition.

Late verge watches in single cases, such as the one we looked at in Chapter 2, **figure 47**, can be much cheaper if you can find one. The trade seems to regard and price these watches very much as a corresponding lever watch of the period. Because of this it is possible to pay as little as £150-£160 for a verge watch albeit in a single case.

English fusee lever watches in working order are still in plentiful supply, a wonderful testament to their makers. It should not be difficult to obtain a standard example in a silver case, similar to the one discussed in Chapter 3 and shown in **figure 48**, for around £140-£160.

Because there are so many of these watches around you should buy only the best examples. Damaged or worn cases should be avoided, and watches with damaged dials should be left alone. Expect to pay a premium for a watch with an unusual or personalised dial like the one shown in **figure 49**. This was the era of the painted watch-dial and these watches are collected in their own right. All dials with painted subjects in the centre are keenly sought after by collectors, especially subjects portraying railway scenes, the new mode of transport of the day!

Swiss lever watches from the late 19th and early 20th centuries, discussed in Chapter 4, are again in plentiful supply, many carrying the retailer's name on the dial. **Figure 50** shows a silver Swiss half-hunter retailed by J W Benson, London.

Although the movements are fairly standard in design, better quality retailers would sometimes (though not always) sell movements with interesting and up-to-date modifications reflecting the some of the advances in watchmaking. Depending on this, an average watch from the period can be bought for around £120-£130. A notable retailer on the dial such as J W Benson may increase the price slightly.

All the watches we have looked at could be regarded as standard watches made simply to tell the time as accurately as possible given the knowledge and ability of the watchmakers of the day. More sophisticated watches were produced to satisfy the customer who wished for a little more information.

These watches not only appealed to the consumer of the day, but also appeal to today's collectors. Naturally as with all items, anything unusual or out-of-the-ordinary tends to push up the price and watches are no exception.

A lot of watches were made with special features—alarm, date and moon-phase, to mention but a few. Always expect to pay a higher price for any extra features that a watch may possess. Of course, the more there is, the more there is to go wrong, and you must be very careful with complicated watches to ensure that the watch is working correctly and check that all the 'bonus' features are in full working order. Specialist repairs are very expensive and rarely can a local person be found to carry out such work. I would always recommend that complicated watches should be bought from a reputable dealer who offers a guarantee.

In reality, the only time you may find a 'bargain' is if the complicated movement is housed in a relatively cheaper case. The quarter-repeater shown in **figure 51** would be an example of this. Normally repeaters are housed in gold and silver cases; this watch is housed in a cheaper gunmetal case, which is worth far less. The movement may not be quite as well finished or as highly jewelled as a corresponding movement in a gold case, but otherwise it functions in the same way. The watch shown in **figure 51** is in good condition and works perfectly.

In a gunmetal case a similar quarter repeater watch could be purchased for around £400; in a silver case with a better movement you could expect to pay £700.

Some of the prices that I have quoted may well be beyond a lot of people, and although the price of watches in working condition may make them expensive, watches in need of repair can be bought more cheaply. If you are not bothered about the watches working, you can assemble a good collection of non-working watches for far less than if they are working. They are just as interesting to look at and the history of the movements and cases is just the same. However as I said earlier, I would caution against buying a broken watch with the idea of a effecting a quick and cheap repair—

Figure 52.

that is, unless you are a watchmaker and know what you are doing. It is tempting, but in reality the cost of commercial repairs tends to rule this out.

Further down the road there is the possibility of collecting watch parts. Many Victorian silver and gold watches were scrapped for the bullion values of their cases, and movements, dials and other parts are frequently encountered on Internet auction sites and at the clock fairs. **Figure 52** shows a collection of pocket watch dials that have been collected and mounted together. Decorative watch cocks from verge watches are also items that are now eagerly collected.

Having amassed a collection of pocket watches, what is the best way of looking after them?

Clearly the watches should be protected from physical harm and not just left lying around or in a drawer. The worst thing that can befall a pocket watch is that it should be dropped on a hard floor. Not only could this damage the case and break the glass, but the movement may also suffer a broken fusee chain or pivot. The watches should also be kept in a dry environment and at room temperature.

Collectors often ask me if they should run their watches or have their watches serviced. Personally I would not advise running an antique pocket watch on a daily basis. I think you must respect the age of the watch and possible worn condition of some of the components. Be content to run the watches infrequently or for demonstration purposes. Never, never, never over-wind pocket watches, especially a fusee movement, and be aware that rear-wound fusee watches are generally wound anti-clockwise. Most antique pocket watches are not run sufficiently to require regular servicing, though the opinion of a professional watch repairer should be sought if you do run your watches regularly or you are in any doubt. A practical examination is really required in order to judge the overall condition of the movement.

CHAPTER 9
Cleaning an American pocket watch

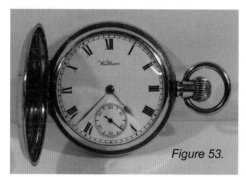

Figure 53.

Figure 54.

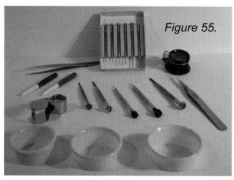

Figure 55.

Not all collectors are interested in the mechanics of their watches or have any desire to dismantle them. Many collect the watches for the visual interest of the dials and cases and never even run their watches. As most mechanical watches require winding every day, for anyone with even a modest collection it would be a bit of a chore to have to wind them all each day.

Most serious collectors do like their watches to work, and with many watches (ones with no mechanical damage) cleaning is all that is required to bring them back to life.

Working on a watch movement is relatively easy. The skill lies in the use of the tools to dismantle and re-assemble the movement. A certain amount of dexterity is required with tweezers and screwdrivers, two of the watchmaker's most important tools!

At all stages during the dismantling and reassembling process do not be afraid to seek the advice of a professional regarding the condition of any components or if you are unsure of any of the procedures. Most watchmakers are only too happy to offer help and encouragement to the beginner who has a genuine interest in watches.

The absolute beginner should never attempt dismantling a small wristwatch. The components are far too delicate and the beginner's skills will not be good enough to cope with them. As an introduction to cleaning a watch the beginner should first dismantle and clean an American pocket watch. For learning purposes this type of watch is ideal.

The Waltham Watch Co (and many other American watchmaking firms) made and exported thousands of quality pocket watches from America around the beginning of the 20th century. They are still in plentiful supply. Many of these watches were cased in less expensive alloy or gold-filled cases and can be purchased relatively cheaply. Earlier English and Swiss pocket watches tend to be cased in more valuable solid gold or silver cases.

Figure 56.

Not only are these earlier watches more expensive, but some of them are perhaps not the easiest to work on for the beginner. That said, American watches are still good quality and of value, and they should be treated with respect. They must not be thought of as dispensable items just to practise on. Every effort should be taken to work on the movements carefully and in a workmanlike manner.

The watch shown in **figure 53** is a Waltham hunter gold-filled Giant model and carries the movement Serial No 19400047, which dates the watch to 1913. The movement is shown in **figure 54**. A watch like this is ideal for the beginner to start with. Not only is the physical size of the movement an advantage, but also, as the parts are interchangeable, it is possible to obtain spare parts from corresponding watches to replace damaged components.

Often damaged or incomplete watches can be bought on the Internet or at the major clock fairs. If you can purchase a damaged watch of the same make and size it is possible to repair and bring another otherwise broken watch back to life. However as usually even the basic models are jewelled to some extent, they usually exhibit very little wear to the vital components, hence a lot of these watches can still be

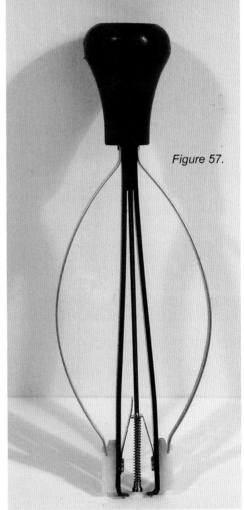

Figure 57.

Figure 58.

bought in working order.

The watch shown in **figure 53** is working, but running erratically and stopping frequently—all symptoms of a dirty movement in need of cleaning and oiling. It is possible for even the beginner to successfully dismantle a simple movement such as this as long as he or she is careful and posses the correct tools and materials. The main differences in the tools used by a watchmaker—as opposed to a clockmaker—is in their size and method of use.

In order to dismantle and clean a simple pocket watch, very few tools are required initially: a selection of quality watchmaker's screwdrivers, a pair of good tweezers, a set of watch oilers and watch oil. Other tools may make the job a little easier, but basically a watch can be dismantled and re-assembled with just a set of screwdrivers and tweezers.

Figure 55 shows a selection of watchmaker's screwdrivers and tweezers, as well as some other items the beginner may find useful. Depending on your eyesight a couple of loupes (eyeglasses) can be of use, as well as an assortment of movement holders. Two oilers are generally all that are necessary, one for oiling the train and the other one for larger component parts.

Figure 56 shows plastic containers for keeping screws and other dismantled components safely together, wooden cocktail sticks used to 'peg out' the pivot holes, and naturally a small phial of watchmaker's oil. A case-opening knife is also shown, most useful when opening the backs of pocket watches or removing the bezels of dials.

The tool shown in **figure 58** is used to remove the sleeves of winding stems from cases. Although when cleaning a movement the winding stem should ideally be removed and lubricated, this is not always necessary. A hand-removing tool is shown in **figure 57**. This is very useful, as will be explained in the next chapter.

A proprietary watch cleaning fluid and rinse will be required but it is not necessary to use a watch-cleaning machine or ultrasonic tank. The cleaning process can be carried out by hand after the movement has been dismantled.

Buy the best screwdrivers and tweezers that you can afford and always look after your watch repairing tools and equipment. Do not just throw them all together in a box or drawer or mix them up with other tools or they may be damaged.

CHAPTER 10
Taking the movement out of the case

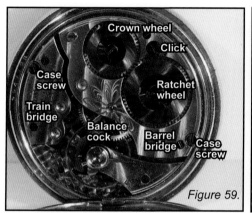

Crown wheel
Click
Case screw
Ratchet wheel
Train bridge
Balance cock
Barrel bridge
Case screw

Figure 59.

Figure 60.

Unlike a clock movement, where nearly all of the wheel train is contained between the front and back plates, most watches have a main or back plate and separate bridges acting as a front plate to keep the wheels in place. This greatly facilitates the assembly and dismantling of the movement, as naturally you only have to concentrate on working with two or three wheels at a time.

Take care to handle the movement and components with your fingers as little as possible. Traces of moisture can encourage rust on the delicate components.

In **figure 59** you can see there are two principal bridges positioning the wheelwork of the watch. One, the barrel bridge, retains the mainspring barrel, crown and ratchet wheel as well as the centre and third wheels. The other, the train bridge, retains the fourth and escape wheels. The balance wheel is retained in place by the balance cock, separate from either of the other two bridges.

When using screwdrivers and tweezers, very little force should be exerted. The correct size of screwdriver should be used relative to the size of the screwhead, and components and screws should be picked up lightly with the tweezers. If the screws are gripped too firmly between the points of the tweezers there is a strong likelihood that they will fly from the tweezers never to be found again. It is a good idea to work over a large white plastic tray with 1in (2.5cm) raised edges. Should a component or screw fall from your tweezers it is a little easier to find this way. Always try to work in an environment where any lost screws or components can be easily found!

The power should be let off before removing any of the bridges or components. With this particular watch this is best done whilst the movement is still in the case. Between the crown wheel and the ratchet wheel there is a small click or pawl operating on the

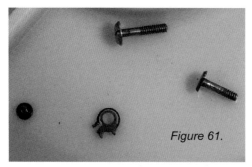

Figure 61.

Figure 62.

Figure 63.

ratchet wheel, **figure 60**. To let down the power of the mainspring this click is removed and the mainspring allowed to unwind in a controlled manner.

Before removing the click, the crown of the winding stem is positioned between the thumb and forefinger and the power of the mainspring taken off the click by winding the crown slightly forwards. The power can then be released by holding the click back off the ratchet with your tweezers and letting the crown *slowly* rotate anticlockwise between the thumb and the forefinger until it stops of its own accord. This should be done carefully. The click screw is then unscrewed and removed from the movement with the tweezers. The click screw is very small indeed and care should be taken not to grip it too tightly in case it springs from the point of the tweezers. Both the click and its screw should be placed in a container for safe keeping. **Figure 61** shows the dismantled click and its screw. The other two screws in the photograph are the case screws, which will be removed later on.

As the different components are dismantled and removed from the watch they should be kept with their relative screws. Although the bridge screws and several of the other movement screws are interchangeable, this is not the case with all movements. It is a good habit to work in a methodical structured way when dismantling a watch movement. By doing this you learn to relate the components, screws and so on to their location on the movement much quicker.

The movement can now be removed from the case.

With most pocket watches the movement is removed through the front of the case. In order to do this the dial bezel is first removed. On this watch the bezel is a press fit and is best taken off with a case knife. The edge of the blade is carefully placed under the edge of the bezel and the bezel is then gently prized off. Hold the case securely in your hand and make sure the knife does not slip marking the bezel or glass. With the bezel and glass removed take care not to catch the dial or hands with your fingers whilst removing the movement.

Figure 64.

The two screws holding the movement in the case are shown in **figures 62** and **63** and are usually the largest screws situated diagonally opposite each other on the back of the movement, right at the edge of the movement and case. The case screws should be removed and the winding stem pulled out. The movement should then be eased out of the case from the top, and placed in a movement holder, **figure 64**, in preparation for removing the hands and dial.

It is most important when dismantling a watch not to mark or damage the dial. Removing the hands is thus best performed with a hand-removing tool like that shown in **figure 57**, which is specially made to remove the hands without damaging the dial, **figures 65** and **66**.

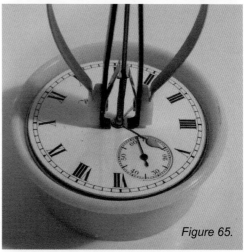

Figure 65.

Figure 66.

You can see the tool has two plastic feet which press against the dial whilst removing the hands, preventing any damage to the enamel. At the same time the tool grips and removes the hands securely. Any attempt at just levering the hands from the dial can result in a damaged dial and lost hands. The hands can be located quite tightly on the cannon pinion and hour wheel and they can fly quite a distance if removed in an uncontrolled manner.

Figure 67.

Figure 68.

Figure 69.

Most dials on this type of watch are held in place with small screws gripping the three dial feet attached to the rear. The screws are located in the periphery of the movement plate and one of the screw heads can be seen in **figure 67**, just under the dial edge. These screws are exceptionally small and great care should be exercised when removing them. Once this has been done, the dial can be gently eased from the movement. Do not be tempted to just ease the screws and leave them in place in the movement plate. During the handling and cleaning process there is the risk they may fall out and be lost.

With the dial removed the movement should be returned to the movement holder, **figure 68**. You can also see the hour and minute wheel in situ on the movement plate and a small springy brass washer just to the left of them. This dial washer is normally situated beneath the dial on the hour wheel in order to keep the hour wheel in place on the cannon pinion.

After taking off the dial I always remove the hour wheel, minute wheel, cannon pinion and dial washer. These items are not fixed in place in any way and may easily fall off, becoming lost or damaged. Whilst the movement is still assembled, place it in a movement holder, **figure 69**. This not only makes the movement easier to work on but also protects it from accidental damage.

Note: *Please bear in mind that not all pocket watch movements are identical. The basic procedures are however the same.*

CHAPTER 11
Dismantling and cleaning the movement

D ismantling a watch movement is relatively easy. However, as it is taken apart it becomes nothing more than a collection of very small wheels and other odd-shaped components. The very thought of reassembling it may be much less appealing!

The beginner is often advised to make a sketch of the parts before dismantling them, however a digital camera can provide a much more accurate record than any rough sketch or drawing. The ability of the camera to zoom in and record different parts of the movement as it is being dismantled can leave no doubt as to the position and relationship of each screw and component, however small, on the movement.

If this is the first time that you have dismantled a watch movement and you own a digital camera, it is a good idea to take a photograph at each stage in the process. You will then be able to remember each stage and identify the location of the components in relation to one another. A series of photographs also will be of use for reference purposes, reminding you of the procedure and familiarising you with the parts of the watch. If a camera is not available then a few sheets of A4 and a pencil will have to suffice.

The first component to be removed is the barrel bridge. Here, this holds the mainspring barrel, centre and third wheels in place. It is screwed to the movement plate with three screws.

The crown wheel is screwed to the bridge and the ratchet wheel locates on a square on the barrel arbor. The watch that I am dismantling is fitted with a safety barrel. Unlike a going barrel, this does not have to be dismantled to remove the barrel arbor. With this

Figure 70.

Figure 71.

watch both the crown and ratchet wheels can be removed after taking the bridge off the plate. In a watch with a going barrel the ratchet wheel should be removed prior to taking off the barrel bridge.

If you are not sure which type of barrel is fitted, remove the crown and ratchet wheels before removing the bridge. One point worth noting: on some movements, left-hand threads are used on the screws holding the crown wheel in place.

With a correct-sized screwdriver, remove the three bridge screws and gently ease the bridge upwards away from the plate. The bridge foot is provided with steady pins to locate it correctly when assembled. When removing any bridge—or the balance cock—always lift it vertically. Never be tempted to tilt the bridge in any way as this could damage or break the fine pivots of the train wheels. As you remove screws and components from the movement put them in a safe container noting their purpose and location on the movement. Never

Figure 72.

Figure 73.

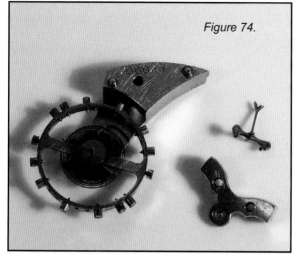

Figure 74.

Figure 75.

just mix all the screws and components together.

Figure 70 shows the movement with the barrel bridge removed. Here you can see the mainspring barrel, and centre and third wheels still in place on the movement plate. The barrel arbor is still attached to the ratchet wheel on the bridge. The centre and third wheels are removed with the tweezers; again the components must be lifted vertically out of their pivot holes. The mainspring barrel is then removed. **Figure 71** shows the plate at this stage.

You will also see that the winding assembly is still in place. This is left until all the other bridges and wheels have been removed. The train bridge and balance cock are still attached to the movement plate, **figure 71**. The train bridge is removed next, freeing the fourth wheel and the escape wheel.

As we work our way up the wheel train you will notice the wheels are getting progressively smaller; more care must be exercised when removing these components.

Figure 72 shows the plate with the train bridge, fourth and escape wheels removed and the balance wheel and balance cock still in place. The screw holding the balance cock is now removed and the balance wheel and cock carefully lifted from the plate. When easing the foot of the balance cock from the plate, be careful not to tip the balance cock and damage the balance wheel pivots. Using the tweezers, ease the balance wheel up and away from the movement. When removed from the plate the balance will hang from the hairspring; the balance cock should be turned over and the pivot of the balance staff located in its pivot hole, **figure 73**.

The only items now left in place should be the winding assembly and the pallets and pallet bridge. The screws holding the pallet bridge in place are very small indeed, and great care must be taken when removing and handling them. With the pallet bridge removed the pallets should be carefully lifted from the plate. Again take care when handling the pallets: these are probably the smallest components of the watch and most delicate to handle. Pay particular attention not to damage the guard pin, the small vertical pin situated behind the fork on the lever.

In **figure 74** you can see the balance wheel, pallets and pallet bridge. There is no need for the beginner to remove the hairspring from the balance or unpin the spring

Figure 76.

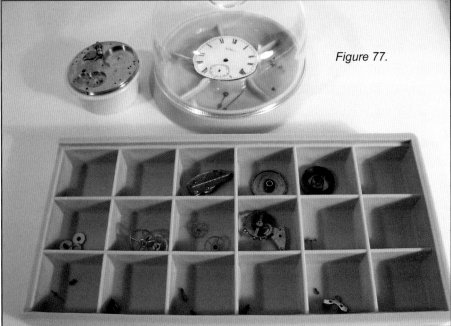

Figure 77.

from its stud on the balance cock. If the hairspring appears damaged in any way the components should be taken to a watchmaker for his opinion.

Whilst the components are to hand they should be inspected with a loupe. Check that the pallet stones on the pallet arm and the impulse stone fitted to the roller table of the balance are not chipped or cracked in any way. Damaged stones should be referred to a watchmaker for advice.

Having removed the all the wheels and the escapement, you should be used to handling small components, as well as being proficient in the use tweezers and screwdrivers. Hopefully, you will have managed not to lose any of the movement screws in the process.

Figure 75 shows the pillar plate and the barrel bridge. Only the winding assembly/ clutch now need to be removed from the plate. The winding assembly comprises a winding arbor or push-pin, winding pinion and winding sleeve. A setting spring operates on the clutch via a setting or clutch lever.

These components can vary from watch to watch, and I strongly recommend that you make a drawing or take photograph of this assembly before you dismantle the components. When re-assembling the watch it is sometimes difficult to remember the precise location and relationship of the components. The positions of the setting spring and lever in particular should be noted. These items are not as delicate as some of the other items removed from the movement, but care should still be exercised when removing them.

When dismantling this particular watch it was not necessary to remove the crown and ratchet wheels prior to removing the barrel bridge. These items should now be unscrewed and taken off. The crown wheel is fairly straightforward to dismantle; again keep the component parts and screws together. On this movement when the screw is removed from the winding ratchet the barrel arbor will come away and this should be placed with the mainspring barrel.

Should the mainspring of a watch break, it is highly likely that the shock that goes through the movement when this happens will damage other wheels or pivots. Over the years watch manufacturers devised various ingenious methods and devices in order to overcome the problem.

On a watch with a conventional going barrel a special safety pinion was usually fitted to the centre wheel. If the mainspring broke the safety pinion would absorb the shock and prevent further damage to the wheel train.

If a safety barrel is fitted to a watch movement a safety pinion is not required. The dismantled safety barrel on this watch is shown in **figure 76**. You can see the spring contained in the barrel and the underside of the top of the barrel, which is also the first or driving wheel of the movement.

On the underside of the wheel you can see a collar, with a small hook, which attaches to the centre of the spring. With a safety barrel the mainspring is attached to the driving wheel and barrel but not to the winding arbor. Both the ratchet wheel and barrel are provided with a square hole, which positively locates on the winding arbor. In effect the winding arbor winds the barrel not the spring, therefore should the spring break, the barrel, winding arbor and ratchet take the impact, not the wheel train.

As the mainsprings on watches are fairly small, it was (and still is) common for some repairers to remove and insert these springs into the barrel by hand. This is bad practice. Watch and clock mainsprings must never be removed or inserted in this way. Not only is it dangerous to the repairer, but the springs may be distorted. They should always be removed and inserted with a mainspring winder. As beginners are not likely to own a mainspring winder the barrel should be taken to a watchmaker to remove and clean the spring. If the spring is found to be fatigued the watchmaker will also be able to obtain a replacement and fit it.

If whilst dismantling the watch attention was paid to keeping the screws and components segregated, the compartments in your work trays should appear similar to those in **figure 77**. With the watch fully dismantled now is a good time to inspect all the components with a loupe. The steelwork—especially the teeth or 'leaves' of the pinions—should be checked for any signs of rust. Any traces of rust should be removed. This is fairly fine work, but it should be possible to remove rust using very fine emery papers and Diamantine polishing powder. Any traces of residual polishing compound should be washed away with paraffin.

Figure 78.

Figure 79.

We can now clean the plates and wheels prior to re-assembly. While the professional watchmaker can easily justify the cost of an ultrasonic tank—the best way to clean a watch—the beginner or amateur will find this hard to justify. Fortunately a dismantled watch can be cleaned by hand.

Commercial watch cleaning fluids have improved substantially over the years and several makes are suitable for hand cleaning. I frequently use Horotech spirit-based cleaner and rinse which I find is very good at dissolving and removing congealed oil, dirt and tarnish.

As watch cases are generally very well made, the movements are protected to some extent from the substantial ingress of dirt and debris. This is not to say that dirt does not find its way into a watch movements which, by virtue of their size, require very little dirt to stop them working. Generally however, periodic light cleaning and oiling will keep a watch movement running for a very long time.

At least two glass beakers or jars will be required, one to hold the cleaning fluid, the other for the rinse. Figure 78 shows two wide-mouthed beakers suitable for the purpose. It is important to use glass beakers so the contents can be seen and no parts accidentally left in the fluids.

Whichever cleaning fluids you use always read the manufacturer's health warnings and recommendations and observe them most carefully.

Rather than placing all the parts in the cleaning solution you may wish to clean the components in batches. This may take a little longer, but a systematic and defined cleaning process means that there is less risk of damaging or losing any of the small components: you count them in and count them out.

Immerse the plates and bridges first. These are relatively heavy items and would easily damage the smaller wheels or pallets if they were included with them. The cleaning solution is agitated periodically with a small brush. This is generally sufficient to remove any old oil and dirt that may be lodged in the pivot holes.

The items are then removed and placed in the rinse solution. Try to transfer as little of the cleaning solution as possible into the beaker containing the rinse. Usually it is recommended that the components be given a second rinse, which should take place in a separate container to the first rinse.

The same procedure is carried out for the train wheels and all the screws and other dismantled parts of the watch. With the smaller components take care when agitating the solution and transferring them from one solution to another. Again, do the cleaning in batches, a few wheels or parts at a time. This way there is less risk of misplacing or mixing up any of the components.

The balance wheel, hairspring and balance cock can be cleaned in the same way. Avoid catching the hairspring when removing the balance from the solution. Hold and manipulate the balance cock carefully with the tweezers. After the parts have been removed from the second rinse they should be placed to dry on blotting paper or absorbent kitchen towel, **figure 79**. This will absorb any surplus fluid and so speed up the drying process. The components should be kept in a warm environment until dry. The pivot holes in the plates and bridges can then be cleaned out with wooden cocktail sticks.

With all the movement cleaned make sure all the components and screws are grouped together for ease of identification and re-assembly. Make sure that you know where all the parts and their relative screws are, and that none of the screws is missing.

CHAPTER 12
Re-assembling the movement

H aving dismantled and cleaned the watch movement it now only remains to re-assemble and oil it before returning it to its case. In the previous chapter I suggested that the beginner take the mainspring barrel to a watchmaker to remove and clean the spring. I presume that this has been done and having cleaned all the components of the watch the parts are now ready for re-assembly.

Re-assembling a watch movement is a little more difficult than taking one apart, primarily because inevitably at certain stages in the assembly you find yourself having to work with and manipulate more than one component at a time. This is where the small sizes of the wheels *etc* can make life a little difficult, and your expertise and skills with the tweezers and screwdriver will be severely tested.

When re-assembling the movement take care to handle the plates and components as little as possible; always use the tweezers to locate the parts.

For the beginner, possibly the best procedure is to re-assemble the watch in the reverse manner to how it was dismantled. There is perhaps more room to work on the small components such as the pallets and escape wheel when there are fewer other components in place on the movement plate.

First, the movement plate should be placed in a movement holder. The winding assembly is the first item to be replaced. If when dismantling the watch you made a drawing and a note of the positions of the various springs and levers *etc* you should have no problems in fitting the assembly in place. The winding stem and setting springs should be lubricated and all the parts of the clutch should operate freely on the stem.

The next item to be replaced is the pallet arm and bridge. Take care when replacing the pallets that they are fitted the right way up, with the guard pin upright. Insert the

Figure 80.

Figure 81.

lower pivot of the pallet arbor in the movement plate, and gently position the bridge in place. With the tweezers, manipulate the pallet arm until both pivots are positively located in their respective pivot holes. Using a loupe check that the upper pivot can be seen protruding through the pivot hole in the bridge. Only if the pivot is visible should the bridge be screwed in place. If the pivots are not located correctly in the plate and bridge you risk breaking the pivots on the arbor. With the bridge in place gently check the freedom of the pallet arm. **Figure 80** shows the movement plate with the winding assembly and pallets fitted in place.

The escape and fourth wheel can now be fitted in place as shown in **figure 81**. The train bridge should then be replaced. Again take care to see the wheels and bridge are properly positioned and that before screwing the bridge in place the upper pivots of the arbors can be seen located in their respective pivot holes in the bridge. With the train bridge in place, the third and centre wheels as well as the mainspring barrel can be placed on the movement plate as shown in **figure 82**.

On this watch the winding arbor is detachable from the barrel. The arbor should now be fitted into the barrel prior to fitting the barrel bridge in place. Take care to ensure that the square of the arbor is positively located in the barrel, and the lower pivot of the arbor is located in its pivot hole. With this type of barrel, the main or first wheel should be lightly oiled where the wheel runs on the arbor. Again always ensure the upper pivots are located correctly before screwing the bridge in place. After replacing the barrel bridge the barrel arbor should be oiled where it runs in the bridge.

With the bridge in place the crown and ratchet wheels can be replaced along with the ratchet click. The ratchet wheel must locate correctly on the square of the winding arbor. The ratchet click should be lightly oiled. **Figure 83** shows the movement at this stage and only the balance wheel requires refitting in place.

With all the wheelwork in place the arbor pivots should be lightly oiled. Do not use too much oil: the oil sinks should not be filled with oil. Capillary action will take the oil down the pivot to the shoulder of the arbor. Too much oil only attracts dust and thickens the oil.

Before fitting the balance in place, the pivot hole in the balance cock should be oiled. The balance staff can be held in the tweezers as shown in **figure 84** in order to access the pivot hole with the oiler. Take care to ensure that no oil comes into contact with the

Figure 82.

Figure 83.

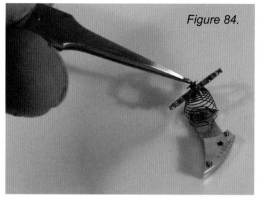

Figure 84.

Figure 85.

hairspring.

The balance wheel is then fitted to the movement. Whilst positioning the balance ensure that the impulse jewel engages between the forks in the pallet arm and that the pivots of the balance staff are located correctly in the movement plate and balance cock. Whilst positioning the balance cock, slightly twist the movement, encouraging the balance to swing; this helps to confirm the pivots are located properly whilst screwing the balance cock in place. The lower balance pivot hole should then be oiled along with the faces of one or two teeth of the escape wheel. It is worth mentioning to the beginner that oil is never applied to the teeth or gears of the wheel train. The only reason a couple of teeth of the escape wheel are oiled is that this is the most practical and accurate means of transferring oil to the acting faces of the pallets. The watch with the balance wheel in place is shown in **figure 85**.

It only now remains to replace the motionwork before fitting the dial and hands in

Figure 86.

Figure 87.

place. The cannon pinion should be placed on the centre arbor and the hour and minute wheels replaced. Both wheels should be lightly lubricated where they run on their respective arbors. With the dial washer placed over the hour wheel the dial can now be replaced.

At this stage take care to ensure that you do not lose any of the dial screws, or in replacing them, drop them into the movement by accident. I have known of several watches having to be dismantled at this late stage in order to find and dislodge a dial screw which fell from the tweezers whilst being replaced.

With the dial fitted in place the hands should be replaced. Take care when working with the seconds hand. This is extremely delicate, and can easily be lost or damaged.

The fully assembled movement can be seen in **figure 86** and the movement reunited with its case in **figures 87** and **88**. The movement should go back into the case without a problem and when the case screws are tightened a check should be made to ensure that the crown and winding stem operate correctly, both in winding up the movement and setting the hands. The hour hand must clear the seconds hand and the minute hand must not catch the hour hand. When replacing the glass and bezel, inspect the rotation of the minute hand to make sure that it clears the glass. If the minute hand is in contact with the glass this can mark the inside of the glass.

I am pleased to say that with this particular watch the dismantling and cleaning process has been worthwhile. The watch is now running well and keeping good time.

Figure 88.

CHAPTER 13
Notes on repairs

Watch repair is a specialist job calling for years of dedicated study and skill. It requires a lot of investment in both time and capital. Most watch components, even in early pocket watches, would not have been made by hand; they may have been hand-finished but would have required the initial machining to have been done on a lathe or wheel-cutting engine. Any damaged components therefore call for professional knowledge and equipment that is usually beyond the reach of the amateur. Also it has to be understood that it is now virtually impossible to obtain spare parts for pocket watches. The main source of supply for component parts has to be other damaged watches which are being sold off for spares.

Does all this mean that the collector or amateur repairer has to make do with watches that either won't go, or face expensive repair bills from the professional watchmaker? A lot depends on the type of watch you decide to collect and what you are personally prepared to accept. Most collectors are happy as long as the watch runs and keeps reasonable time; others (perhaps more optimistic!) are much more demanding and strive for perfect timekeeping.

If you are going to collect older and more valuable early 18th century verge pocket watches these will already have had a long life and will no doubt have been repaired a number of times in the past. Owing to their intrinsic value, the experienced watchmaker who specialises in the restoration of antique pocket watches is perhaps best placed to repair these watches. When buying early watches the mechanical condition of the watch should be checked very thoroughly and unless a reputable dealer offering a guarantee regarding the performance and condition of the movement is selling the watch, do not expect too much in the way of reliability and accuracy. With early 18th century watches you should be perfectly happy if the watch goes and keeps reasonable time for its age.

As with most types of watch movement it is possible to buy uncased movements on which the amateur can learn, providing valuable experience in dismantling and assembling the movements. The English fusee lever watch is still in plentiful supply and here the scope for repair or replacing damaged parts from other movements is much wider. Again redundant, damaged movements are the chief source of supply for spare parts. It is even possible to replace damaged wheels from another movement provided that the diameters and wheel count is the same and the depthing of the teeth is correct.

Bent arbors can be straightened and sometimes it is even possible to straighten bent pivots provided that they have been correctly softened beforehand. Needless to say these are all repairs not to be undertaken lightly and it is as well to practise on spare components until you are confident and proficient. Broken balance staff pivots are best handed to the professional with the correct tools and experience.

Broken or fatigued mainsprings can be replaced with a new spring of the same height and thickness obtained from the material suppliers. The spring should be fitted with a mainspring winder. Winding the spring by hand distorts it and can lead to erratic timekeeping.

If you have nimble fingers and exceptional eyesight even broken fusee chains can be repaired provided that the hooks are in good condition. Again, replacements can be used from other redundant movements, which is perhaps the less frustrating and time-consuming option. Modern replacement jewels are obtainable from the material suppliers but are not always compatible with old movements; again it is possible to re-use jewels from other similar movements. Kinked or damaged balance springs must be replaced with springs of the correct strength and size. It is becoming very difficult to obtain these now from the material suppliers and again old springs can be re-used if in good condition.

With late 19th and early 20th century Swiss, American, lever and cylinder watches the mass-production and interchangeability of parts means that it is much easier to source spare parts for these movements. Also, as the watches are not so old, it is possible to find many still in good working condition. However, do not expect a good rate of time from the small Swiss cylinder fob watch so popular with ladies at the turn of the century. The cylinders on these watches are usually now very badly worn and hence many are now incapable of good timekeeping. Any watches with complicated movements such as a quarter repeater or movements with rare escapements must be handed to the professional for expert attention.

Dismantling and cleaning an American watch movement as show in Chapters 10 to 12 is not beyond the capabilities of the amateur, and is a very good way for the beginner to familiarise himself with the components of a watch movement. As your interest and experience grows and if you start to tackle repairs other specialist tools will be required.

A mainspring winder is essential in order to safely and efficiently wind the mainspring into the barrel. Eventually a watchmaker's lathe will be found essential. This, along with its accessories, is a very expensive piece of equipment, hard for the amateur to justify on the ground of cost, but it will be found that some jobs are impossible to do without one. For this reason many amateur repairers 'farm out' turning or re-pivoting jobs. A staking tool is another very useful but expensive piece of equipment, very accurate and efficient in use, but again hard to justify for the amateur in terms of its cost. Sometime these items can be bought second-hand, but owing to their high cost they are seldom cheap and quickly snapped up.

Watch repairing is a very therapeutic and relaxing hobby and it is surprising what even the amateur can do. He or she is not charging out labour at an hourly rate and can take weeks or even months to complete a repair which would not be viable for a professional to contemplate.

Always treat the watches you are working on with respect and if the job is beyond your capabilities do not be afraid to consult a professional. It may be that you do not possess the skills or equipment to repair the movement properly at the moment, but always remember that as your skills improve the repair may be possible at a later date. Always read up on the mechanism that you are working on and take photographs or make sketches of the layout of the movement if you are not familiar with it.

There are several very good books on the market for the would-be watch repairer to consult. A list of recommended books is given in Appendix 2.

Finally as the keen amateur progresses he or she may consider one of the many courses organised by the British Horological Institute. The courses are run by specialist repairers/restorers dealing with many different aspects of watch repair and are open to members and non-members alike.

APPENDIX 1
Glossary

Arbor. Axle or shaft which carries a *wheel* or *pinion*.

Balance cock. Removable bracket that locates the *balance wheel*.

Balance wheel. Oscillating *wheel* which, in conjunction with the *balance spring*, controls the timekeeping of the *movement*.

Balance spring. Spiral spring controlling the oscillation of the *balance wheel*.

Balance staff. *Arbor* on which the *balance wheel* is fitted.

Bar (or Geneva bar) movement. *Movement* with removable *cocks*, each one retaining an individual *arbor* in place.

Bimetallic balance. See *'Compensating balance'*.

Beat. Oscillation or swing of the *balance wheel* relative to the audible tick of the watch. When the ticks are even the watch is said to be 'in beat'.

Bezel. Ring holding the watch glass in place on the front of the case.

Bridge. Removable *plate* supporting movement *arbors*, usually held in place by two screws.

Broach. Five-sided cutting tool used to enlarge *pivot* holes prior to *re-bushing*.

Bush. Brass tube inserted into the *plate* to correct worn *pivot* holes.

Cannon pinion. *Motionwork pinion* located on and driven by the centre *arbor*, with a pipe that carries the minute hand.

Centrifugal governor. Speed control relying on centrifugal force to regulate the speed of other components.

Centre arbor. *Arbor* on which the *centre wheel* runs.

Centre wheel. Wheel in the train that drives the *cannon pinion*, making one revolution clockwise every hour.

Click. Steel pawl used in conjunction with a *ratchet wheel*.

Clickspring. Spring which bears on the *click* allowing movement but returning the *click* into place.

Cock. Separate bracket or support usually held in place on the *movement plate* with a single screw.

Compensating balance. Bi-metallic *balance* which compensates for changes in temperature.

Contrate wheel. *Wheel* with teeth cut at right angles in the rim.

Countersink. Enlarged upper part of a hole.

Crown wheel. *Escape wheel* in a *verge escapement* or a *wheel* with teeth at right angles to the plane.

Cylinder escapement. *Escapement* where a cylindrical *balance staff* doubles as the *escapement pallets*.

Dead-beat escapement. *Escapement* without *recoil*.

Depthing. Name given to the optimum meshing of the *wheels* and *pinions* in a wheel train.

Dial. Face of watch.

Drop. In an *escapement* the interval between the release of one tooth on the *escape wheel* and the arrest of another.

Dust cap. A removable metal cover fitted to the back of the watch to prevent dust entering the *movement*

Endshake. Free movement between the *arbors* and *plates* in a watch *movement*.

Engine turning. Decorative finish given to watch cases and *movement plates*.

English lever escapement. *Escapement* utilising a *lever* to impulse the *balance wheel*, with the lever and pallets situated at right angles to the *escape wheel*, layout greatly favoured by English watchmakers.

Escapement. Mechanism that *impulses* the *balance wheel* and regulates the rate at which the *movement* runs.

Escape wheel. The final *wheel* in the *going train* which *impulses* the *balance wheel*.

Frictional rest escapement. *Escapement* in which the *balance* is in almost constant contact with other components of the *escapement*, for example a *verge escapement*.

Full-plate. Watch *movement* with only one removable *plate*.

Fusee. *Movement* component with a conical shape and groove for the *fusee chain*, to even out the torque of the *mainspring* as it unwinds.

Fusee chain. Chain connecting the *fusee* to the *mainspring* barrel.

Going barrel. Brass barrel that contains the *mainspring* and drives the *movement*. The teeth are attached or cut into the wall or periphery of the *barrel*.

Going train. Series of connecting *wheels* and *pinions* which deliver power to the *escapement* and drive the *motionwork* and the hands of the watch.

Gold filled. Gold bonded to a base metal such as brass.

Great wheel. First *wheel* in the wheel train.

Guard pin. Vertical pin behind the fork on the lever of the *escapement*.

Hairspring. See 'Balance spring'.

Half-plate. Watch with two separate removable *plates* for different *wheels* of the train.

Hour wheel. *Wheel* which runs on the *cannon pinion* and on which the hour hand is fitted. The hour wheel gears with the minute *wheel/pinion* and makes one revolution clockwise every 12 hours.

Impulse. Force provided by the *movement* in order to keep the *balance wheel* oscillating.

Intermediate wheel. In the *going train* the second *wheel* in the train to the going *barrel* or *great wheel*.

Leaf. Tooth of a *pinion*.

Lever escapement. Escapement using a lever to *impulse* the *balance wheel*.

Lifting lever. Levers used and arranged to activate other components.

Jewels. *Pivot* bearings made from ruby or other normally synthetic gemstone material.

Keyless. Watch wound without a key.

Mainspring. Coiled spring providing power to the *movement*.

Maintaining power. Means of keeping *movement* running while being wound.

Minute wheel/pinion. A combined wheel and pinion forming part of the *motionwork*: the minute wheel gears with the *cannon pinion* and the minute wheel pinion gears with the *hour wheel* in order to provide the 12:1 reduction required for the *hour hand*.

Motionwork. *Wheels* and *pinions* used to obtain the 12:1 reduction in gearing for the hour hand, and to ensure both hands turn in the same direction. Motionwork is separate from the *going train* of the *movement*.

Movement. The mechanism.

Pair case. A watch with literally two cases, an inner and separate outer case.

Pallets. A pair of specially shaped steel teeth that intercept with the teeth of the *escape wheel* at a regular interval.

Pillars. Metal bars holding the *plates* apart.

Pinion. A small wheel usually attached to an *arbor* having fewer than 20 teeth, typically six to twelve.

Pivot. Ends of the *arbor* which have been reduced in diameter and run in the watch *plates*.

Plates. Flat brass sheets drilled to accept *wheel* and *pinion arbors*.

Push-piece. A button pressed to activate other components.

Rack. Toothed component used to determine the number of hours struck.

Ratchet wheel. *Wheel* with teeth cut at a steep angle. Used in conjunction with a steel *click* and return spring to ensure the *wheel* travels in one direction only.

Re-bushing. Process of inserting a brass *bush* in a *plate* to repair a worn *pivot* hole.

Recoil. Backward motion of a tooth on the *escape wheel* when arrested by the *pallet*.

Recoil escapement. E*scapement* in which the *escape wheel* is momentarily driven backwards as the escape wheel teeth alternately encounter the *pallets*.

Regulator. Lever or device used to regulate the timekeeping of the watch

Repeater. Watch which audibly strikes the approximate time when a button on the side of the case is depressed.

Snail. Snail-shaped device found on a rack striking *movement* that controls the number of hours struck by the watch.

Stem wind. System used to wind and set the hands of a *keyless* watch.

Swiss lever. Escapement utilising a lever to *impulse* the *balance wheel*, much favoured by Continental and American watchmakers: the lever, *pallets* and *escape wheel* are laid out in a straight line.

Third wheel. *Wheel* in the *going train* between the *centre wheel* and *escape wheel*.

Three-quarter plate. Watch with separate *plates* for different *wheels* of the *going train*.

Timing screws. Two or four adjustable screws fitted to the ends of the *balance* arms.

Timepiece. Watch that tells the time but does not strike or chime.

Verge. *Balance staff* carrying the *pallets* on a *verge escapement*.

Verge escapement. Early *frictional rest escapement* employing a *crown wheel*.

Wheel. Watch gear usually made from brass with more than 20 teeth.

Winding arbor. Squared end of an *arbor* designed to accept a key and wind the *movement*.

APPENDIX 2
Further reading

The following books will provide further reading for the amateur watch repairer. Unfortunately some of the books may now be out of print, but may still be obtainable from some libraries or good horological booksellers dealing in new and second-hand books.

WATCH & CLOCK MAKING AND REPAIRING by W J Gazeley.
CLOCK & WATCH REPAIRING by Donald de Carle.
PRACTICAL WATCH REPAIRING by Donald de Carle.
REPAIRING OLD CLOCKS & WATCHES by Anthony J Whiten.
MECHANICAL & QUARTZ WATCH REPAIR by Mick Watters.
COLLECTING & REPAIRING WATCHES by Max Cutmore.
THE POCKET WATCH HANDBOOK by Max Cutmore.
WATCH AND CLOCK ESCAPEMENTS by W J Gazeley.
WATCH REPAIRERS MANUAL by H B Fried.